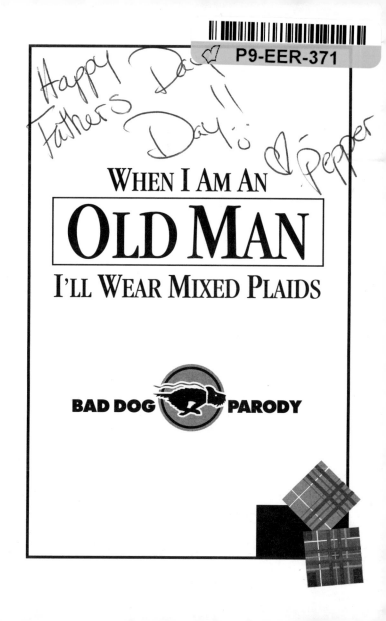

Happy Fathers Day!! Day!❤ ❤ Pepper

P9-EER-371

WHEN I AM AN

OLD MAN

I'LL WEAR MIXED PLAIDS

BAD DOG **PARODY**

Bad Dog Press
P.O. Box 130066
Roseville, MN 55113

World Wide Web address: http://www.octane.com

When I Am An Old Man I'll Wear Mixed Plaids

First printed in 1996

Printed in the United States of America.

96 97 98 99 00   10 9 8 7 6 5 4 3 2

Text: Tony Dierckins and Tim Nyberg
Illustrations: Tim Nyberg

ISBN 1-887317-10-4
Library of Congress Catalog Card Number: 96-084860

Warning: *Contains humor, a highly volatile substance if used improperly. Harmful if swallowed. All content is a fictional product of the authors' imaginations. Any resemblance between characters portrayed herein and actual persons living, dead, or residing in New Jersey is purely coincidental. Contents under pressure. Do not use near open flame. Do not use as a flotation device, or at least avoid any situations in which you would need to rely on a book as a flotation device. Any typographic errors are purely intentional and left for your amusement. Always say no to drugs and, by all means, stay in school.*

To our Dads:

Two old men who know we couldn't have gotten away with this kind of crap back in their day, when a man had to work for a living.

— Tony and Tim

WHEN I AM AN OLD MAN...

I'll have time to read the
Preface

You probably received this book as a gift. If so, take note that at least one person in your life thinks of you as an "old man." It doesn't matter if you're 65, 75, 85, or 105—it doesn't even matter if you're only 40—someone's trying to tell you that there's more snow on the roof than fire in the furnace, whatever the halibut that's supposed to mean.

Don't feel bad. The spoiled little whipper-snappers who gave this to you probably didn't have to walk five miles in the snow to get to school like you and I did—what do they know? There's nothing wrong with being old, least not as far as I can see. Being an "old man" gives you lots of freedom: the kind of liberty that comes with not giving a ding-dang about what other people think.

I'm not sure if this freedom is brought on by a chemical change in the brain, male menopause, or overexposure to "Matlock" reruns. All I know is I gathered a whole mess of data with the studies conducted by my firm, the Atrick And Associates Research Group (or AAARG*), and I found a lot of it darn interesting.

I also know that there's a very successful series of books for women that began with *When I'm an Old Woman, I Shall Wear Purple*—the wife has the whole darn set. I figured it's time for us old men to have a book that celebrates us, too—one that gives us permission to do things the way we want. After all, we're going to do it our own way, anyhow. We might as well feel good about it.

— Jerry Atrick

p.s.
And one more thing. I've been hearing a lot these days about how "senility" isn't exactly a "politically correct" word any more—that we should say "dementia." Well senility was good enough for us during the Depression and W.W. II, and I'll be dang-blammed if it ain't good enough for us now!

> The supportive data found in the gray boxes were provided by the Atrick And Associates Research Group (AAARG*).

* *Not to be confused with any auto club, senior citizen's advocate group, or a cliiché exclamation used by pirates.*

vi

WHEN I AM AN OLD MAN...

...I'll wear
mixed plaids.

85.3% of men over the age of 60
wear at least two different patterns
of plaid on any given day, a
tendency that begins shortly after
their 40th birthday.

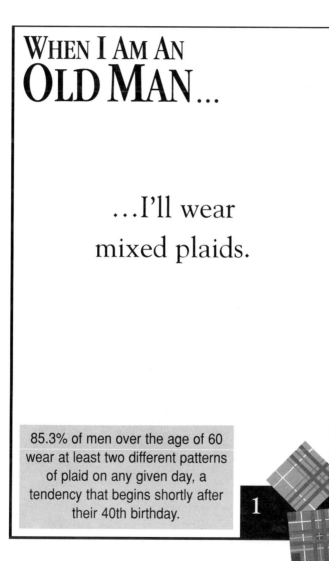

WHEN I AM AN OLD MAN...

...I'll put my
teeth in only when
I need them.

WHEN I AM AN OLD MAN...

...I'll proudly
and loudly
produce massive
amounts of phlegm
at will.

Pharmaceutical manufacturers
have spent millions of dollars trying
to pin down the source of the
older male's ability to naturally
produce effective expectorants.

3

WHEN I AM AN OLD MAN...

...I'll wake up at 5 A.M. even if I have nothing to do because I fell asleep in front of the TV at 7 P.M.

4

WHEN I AM AN OLD MAN...

...I'll fall asleep in my chair in front of the TV by 7 P.M. because I've been up since 5 A.M. —what's your excuse?

Recliner sales to men over the age of 35 increases at the rate of 5% for every 3.5 years of age. By the age of 70, 100% of all men own recliners.

WHEN I AM AN OLD MAN...

...I'll drive as
slow as I want—
I was here first,
wasn't I?

Average speed of drivers
over 60 actually decreases
exponentially with every year they
age. By the time drivers reach 85,
it could take up to three days for
them to back out of a driveway.

WHEN I AM AN OLD MAN...

...I'll buy my
grandchildren gifts
my kids don't
want them
to have.

7

WHEN I AM AN OLD MAN...

...I'll watch
more golf
on TV.

8

WHEN I AM AN OLD MAN...

...I'll score my
golf game
any way I
want to.

The older a man is, the better his
chances are to "shoot his age"—
a temptation that often leads male
golfers to devise an intricate
system of justifications in order
to take certain liberties with
the score card.

WHEN I AM AN OLD MAN...

...I'll rinse my dentures in my coffee cup and then complain, "This coffee tastes like crap!"

10

WHEN I AM AN OLD MAN...

...I'll let waiters and waitresses *really* know how "everything" is tonight.

Because it is the easiest English word to say with a full mouth, 83% of younger folks simply reply "fine" when a waitperson asks, "And how is everything tonight?"

11

WHEN I AM AN
OLD MAN...

...I'll wear
Vicks Vap-o-Rub,®
BenGay,® and that
Icy Blue® stuff
instead of cologne.

12

WHEN I AM AN OLD MAN...

...I'll talk more
and listen less.

This change—which occurs
gradually over a male's entire life—
is the result of becoming more and
more confirmed in his belief that
"I **know** I'm right—no matter what
the 'experts' say."

13

WHEN I AM AN OLD MAN...

...I'll darn-sure let people know what I think about "the crap those kids are listening to on the radio these days."

While 82% of men over 70 claim to hate any *popular* music recorded after 1959, this same group admits to enjoying certain Beatles' songs because the tunes remind them of "a soothing ride in an elevator."

14

WHEN I AM AN OLD MAN...

...I'll watch reruns of "Matlock" and "Murder She Wrote" not because I enjoy them, but because they have at least one character my age that I can relate to.

15

WHEN I AM AN OLD MAN...

...I'll keep driving long after I am physically capable.

16

WHEN I AM AN OLD MAN...

...I'll talk loudly
in restaurants
about my double
hernia operation.

When dining out with their children's in-laws, 68% of retired men feel "compelled" to discuss surgical procedures they have undergone, particularly those in the body's "southern" region.

17

WHEN I AM AN OLD MAN...

...I'll start more sentences with "Whatever happened to..."

18

WHEN I AM AN
OLD MAN...

...I'll let my
gut stick out.
Way out.
Way, way out—
who gives a rip
anymore?

By age 70, 63% of all men
(married and single) don't really
care what they look like, just
as long as they're comfortable
and can get a little peace and
quiet once in a while.

19

WHEN I AM AN OLD MAN...

...I'll eat breakfast
before 6 A.M.,
lunch by 10:30 A.M.,
and dinner
at 3:00 P.M.

WHEN I AM AN OLD MAN...

...I'll spend more time in the drugstore and doctor's office, whether I like it or not.

Since people age 65 and older spend an average of five hours per week reading magazines in waiting rooms, seniors citizens have become the most well read and best informed members of society.

Jerry Atrick Asks:

Are You Wearing Too Many Plaids?

Follow this handy guide and stay plaid appropriate:

A Avoid plaid hats and caps, except those that match your golf pants.

B Plaid vests are okay only at Scottish family get-togethers, but stick to your clan's tartan to avoid clashing with your kilt.

C Lumberjack? Alternative rock star? Cold? If you answered "no," change out of that plaid shirt.

D Plaid boxers okay at any time IF you can manage to keep them hidden.

E Plaid pants only allowed on golf courses.

F If those socks aren't argyle, follow Rule D as it applies to boxers.

ACCESSORIES:
If you must accessorize in plaid (*i.e.*, a tie or handkerchief), eliminate plaids elsewhere.

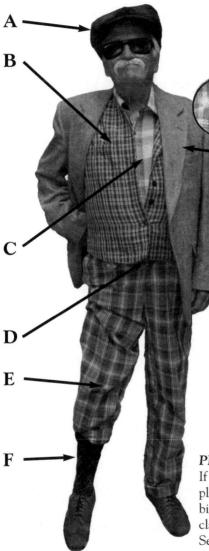

A

B

C

D

E

F

CAUTION: Many fabrics (especially those made in Scotland) include plaids that are virtually imperceptible to the naked eye. However, when viewed under a magnifying device, they are obviously plaid in design and therefore will clash with other, more blatant plaid materials.

PLAID SHOES: If you own a pair of plaid shoes, you have bigger problems than a clashing ensemble. Seek professional help.

WHEN I AM AN
OLD MAN...

...I'll darn-sure
let people know
what I think about
"the crap they're
showing on the
TV these days."

24

Surprisingly, 72% of men over 60
are big fans of "F•R•I•E•N•D•S,"
but they call it "that show with
them three perky gals."

WHEN I AM AN OLD MAN...

...I'll go to
the barber shop
when I don't even
need a haircut.

25

WHEN I AM AN OLD MAN...

...I'll back out
of the driveway
without looking.

This phenomenon was once
thought to be related to the
tendency of drivers in rural
areas to pull onto highways
without checking for cross traffic,
but that habit actually begins
when a boy or girl first learns to
operate farm equipment.

26

WHEN I AM AN OLD MAN...

...I'll let my grandchildren get away with things I used to punish my children for doing.

WHEN I AM AN OLD MAN...

...I'll start more sentences with "Back in my day..."

28

WHEN I AM AN
OLD MAN...

...I'll blow my
nose as hard
and as loud
as I want!

The majority of men over 70
actually look forward to clearing
their nasal passages as this
activity is one of the few things
they can do with the same
vigor as in their prime.

29

WHEN I AM AN OLD MAN...

...I'll make darn
sure I get my
"Senior" discount!

30

WHEN I AM AN OLD MAN...

...I'll forget
what I was
like when
I was their age.

Actually, many older men simply
forget what everything was like
in their day, supplementing their
memory loss by mentally inserting
themselves as the romantic
male lead in old films starring
Lana Turner, Ava Gardner,
and Lauren Bacall.

31

WHEN I AM AN OLD MAN...

...I'll own clothes
—especially jackets—
that match my wife's.

By the tenth year of marriage, 82% of couples begin to look alike. By their 25th anniversary, they begin to dress alike. After fifty years of marriage, they become indistinguishable. The percentage of matching outfits among couples increases dramatically (and begins at a younger age) if the pair enjoy country music line dancing or clogging, or belong to a recreational vehicle travel club.

WHEN I AM AN OLD MAN...

...I'll let my
grandchildren play
with my teeth.

33

WHEN I AM AN OLD MAN...

...I'll darn-sure
let people know
what I think about
"the crap they're
putting in movies
these days."

34

Despite this, 67% of old men are
still willing to sit through any
movies featuring Sharon Stone,
Kim Bassinger, or Uma Thurman.

WHEN I AM AN OLD MAN...

...I'll wheeze when I laugh.

Actually, most old men wheeze when they do just about anything, especially if they've just sat through a movie featuring Sharon Stone, Kim Bassinger, or Uma Thurman.

35

WHEN I AM AN
OLD MAN...

...I'll buy a
Winnebago and
drive it slow enough
to back up highway
traffic for miles.

Highway safety officials have found that for every foot of vehicle over ten feet in length, a senior's speed decreases 4.2 miles per hour. Many seniors driving large recreational vehicles towing boats never exceed 33 m.p.h.

36

WHEN I AM AN OLD MAN...

...I'll schedule my
meals according
to when I take my
medication.

37

WHEN I AM AN
OLD MAN...

...I'll start saying
things like
"It used to be that
when you paid more
than $5,000 for
something, it came
with a basement!"

WHEN I AM AN OLD MAN...

...I'll refuse to stand in long grocery store lines to pay for a quart of milk and a box of bran. If they catch me, I'll just act senile.

The senility defense has become an increasingly popular strategy for law benders in their golden years, especially after Ronald Reagan used it to explain his ignorance of the Iran-Contra Affair.

WHEN I AM AN
OLD MAN...

...I'll lose what
little ability I once
had to distinguish
between navy blue
and black socks.

Actually, most men of all ages
are never fully able to tell the
difference between black and navy
blue footwear; in fact 72% of
widowers say they would remarry if
only so that they'd have someone
to help pick out their clothes.

40

WHEN I AM AN OLD MAN...

...I'll suddenly realize that my legs became skinnier at the same rate my stomach became larger.

41

Jerry Atrick Presents
The Stages of Man

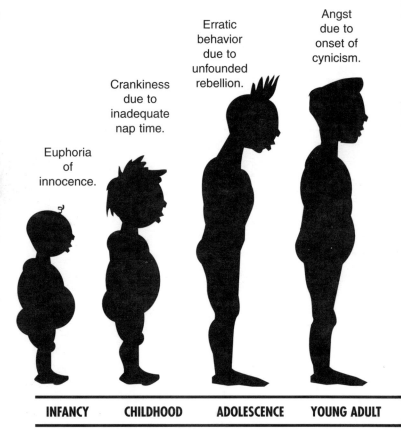

Euphoria of innocence.

Crankiness due to inadequate nap time.

Erratic behavior due to unfounded rebellion.

Angst due to onset of cynicism.

INFANCY   **CHILDHOOD**   **ADOLESCENCE**   **YOUNG ADULT**

The insight expressed on this spread actually describes the phenomenon wherein all men, upon becoming fathers, begin developing what scientists call "big dad stomachs and little dad legs."

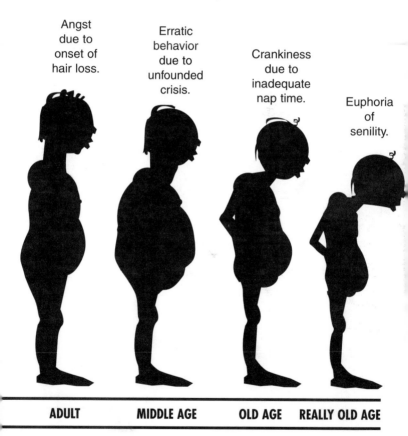

Angst due to onset of hair loss.

Erratic behavior due to unfounded crisis.

Crankiness due to inadequate nap time.

Euphoria of senility.

ADULT   **MIDDLE AGE**   **OLD AGE**   **REALLY OLD AGE**

43

WHEN I AM AN OLD MAN...

...I'll darn sure let people know what I think about "the crap the government makes us go through just to get what we have coming to us."

The majority of retired men also feel that welfare should be cut, not because it isn't a valuable system but because of the long lines on the first of the month when they're trying to cash their social security checks.

44

WHEN I AM AN OLD MAN...

...I'll go to the same restaurant on the same day every week and order the same thing every time.

WHEN I AM AN OLD MAN...

...I'll keep my
turn signal on
as long as I want,
dab nabit!

Sociologists remain perplexed over why older people tend to leave their turn signals on and, sadly, have as yet found no connection between this phenomenon and the fact that 93% of all people native to rural areas have never used their car's signals to indicate a turn!

WHEN I AM AN OLD MAN...

...I'll pass gas
whenever and
wherever I
dang well please.

47

WHEN I AM AN OLD MAN...

...I'll start saying,
"It used to be,
a man had to work
for a livin'!"

WHEN I AM AN OLD MAN...

...I'll start sleeping in one of the kids' old rooms so my snoring doesn't keep the wife up all night.

A study is underway at the University of Arizona at Sun City to find out why 79% of retirement-age couples sleep in separate beds—often in separate rooms—yet these same couples have also purchased side-by-side cemetery plots, usually under a large oak tree.

WHEN I AM AN OLD MAN...

...I'll develop
an addiction to
Milk of Magnesia.®

WHEN I AM AN OLD MAN...

...I'll start
nodding off
in church more.

Actually, by the time they reach 70,
most men start nodding off more
often wherever they are, and when
"caught napping," almost half
automatically respond by saying
"I wasn't sleepin'—I was just
restin' my eyes."

51

WHEN I AM AN
OLD MAN...

...I'll suddenly
find polyester
leisure suits
irresistibly
appealing.

52

Recent government funding
includes a research grant to
examine the possible connection of
the wearing of polyester to senility.

WHEN I AM AN OLD MAN...

...I'll write
long letters to the
editor about whatever
I don't like.

53

WHEN I AM AN OLD MAN...

...I'll darn-sure let people know what I think about "the crap they're printing in the newspapers these days."

Interestingly, this tendency increases dramatically with every letter to the editor that goes unpublished, yet does not decrease when letters are printed.

WHEN I AM AN OLD MAN...

...I'll chug Metamucil® like I used to chug beer.

55

WHEN I AM AN
OLD MAN...

...I'll park in handicapped spots even if they haven't granted me one of them little blue and white tags yet—with this dang sciatica, I've earned it!

56

WHEN I AM AN OLD MAN...

...I'll sit in
the park and
mutter to myself.

This behavior, once thought to
be the result of senility, has
been identified as a defensive
technique used by older men so
that "I don't get none of them
kooks sittin' next to me when
I'm enjoying a little peace
and quiet for once!"

57

WHEN I AM AN
OLD MAN...

...I'll talk about how rough I had it "when I was growing up."

Once people hit 60, they begin to believe that they grew up impoverished during the Great Depression, a fact that will become increasingly interesting when Boomers reach retirement age.

58

WHEN I AM AN
OLD MAN...

...I'll obsessively
make elaborate
contraptions to keep
the dang squirrels
off my bird feeders.

WHEN I AM AN OLD MAN...

...I'll wear black (or navy blue) socks with shorts.

This phenomenon also occurs among fathers of all ages—especially those with particularly white legs—who insist on accompanying their more easily embarrassed children to the beach.

WHEN I AM AN OLD MAN...

...I'll have more
hair growing out
of my nose and ears
than on the top
of my skull.

61

Jerry Atrick's Guide to Inoffensive Cussing

A lifetime of watching your language can lead to some interesting vocabulary choices. Try some of these the next time you feel the need to express yourself in mixed company or at a church social:

- Dang blammit!
- Dab nabbit!
- Darn-tootin'!
- Dadgummit!
- Just a ding-dang minute!
- Who gives a rip?
- I don't give a rat's patooti!
- For cryin' out loud!
- For Pete's sake! (or "for the love of Pete")
- For cat's sake!
- Heck!
- What the halibut!

!*@¿#%¡

AAARG-sanctioned euphemisms for "privates":

- your "southern region"
- where "the sun don't shine"
- what's "in your BVDs" (or "britches")
- "package" or "unit"
- "the equipment"
- "keester" (south end when you're headin' north)

AAARG-sanctioned options for the "F" word:

- friggin'
- fargin'
- frackin'
- freakin'
- boink

Don't Forget!

In order to show that you in no way wish to offend present company, immediately follow each of the statements above with "Pardon my French."

WHEN I AM AN OLD MAN...

…I'll darn-sure let
people know what
I think about
"the crap they're
passing off as
'Made in America.'"

WHEN I AM AN OLD MAN...

...I'll fix broken stuff however I want to.

By the time they reach 45, most men feel they have either performed enough household repairs or watched enough Bob Vila to fix or build just about anything without the benefit of instructions. Consequently, 87% of all printed instructions reach the wastebasket without ever being read.

65

WHEN I AM AN OLD MAN...

...I'll loudly proclaim:
"I've been drivin'
for over fifty years
and I never had to
take any stupid test!"

47% of the times a male over 65
makes the above statement,
he also adds, "And I ain't gonna
take no stupid test just because
some punk kid didn't see me
backin' outta my own dang
driveway, Officer!"

66

WHEN I AM AN OLD MAN...

...I'll tell the same
joke over and over
again and laugh
in earnest each
time I reach the
punch line.

67

WHEN I AM AN OLD MAN...

...I'll loudly state:
"You couldn't get
away with crap like
that in my day."

68

WHEN I AM AN OLD MAN...

...I'll lose
my glasses more.

Most men over the age of 60 own
over four pairs of glasses, yet at
any given moment have no idea
where three of them may be.

WHEN I AM AN
OLD MAN...

…I'll spend hours looking for those glasses when they're perched on the top of my head the whole time.

WHEN I AM AN OLD MAN...

...I'll flirt with women who wouldn't have gone out with me even when I was their age.

Failing eyesight coupled with a tendency to lose glasses and to own old, fading mirrors has been shown to increase self-esteem and confidence in 67% of men over 60.

71

WHEN I AM AN
OLD MAN...

…I'll own
—and wear—
a white belt or
white dress shoes.

Of all men over 60 who retire to
Florida or Arizona, 78% purchase
a clothing ensemble featuring a
white belt and white dress shoes
before they even finish unpacking.

WHEN I AM AN OLD MAN...

...I'll brush my
eyebrow hair
up over my
bald spot.

73

WHEN I AM AN OLD MAN...

...I'll get me one
of them
"ask me about my
grandchildren"
bumper stickers...

74

WHEN I AM AN OLD MAN...

...and if someone asks about my grandkids, I'll tell them to mind their own dang business.

While most seniors become quite protective when strangers inquire about their grandchildren, most feel it's really not a big hassle compared to questions inspired by their "Ask Me About My Various Health-Failing Maladies" bumper sticker.

WHEN I AM AN OLD MAN...

...I'll get me a big ol' Cadillac or Lincoln— I don't care if I can't see over the steering wheel or reach the pedals any more, I've earned the biggest car I can find!

WHEN I AM AN OLD MAN...

...I'll meet my
buddies at the café
every morning
at 10 A.M. for a
cup of coffee and
a caramel roll.

78% of retired men develop and/
or retain similar rituals even long
after they consider even their
best friends "cranky-old-dried-
up-boring sots."

77

WHEN I AM AN
OLD MAN...

...I'll go to them
all-you-can-eat
buffet lunch places
and bring a
doggy bag with me.

WHEN I AM AN OLD MAN...

...I'll turn my hearing aid off so I don't have to listen to my wife tell me how I'm drivin' her nuts.

Physicians have found that most older men get over their vanity concerning hearing aids after the first time they form the sentence, "I didn't hear you—my hearing aid was off."

79

WHEN I AM AN OLD MAN...

...I'll drive my wife
nuts by puttering
around the
house all day.

80

WHEN I AM AN OLD MAN...

...I'll drive my wife nuts by not puttering around the house at night anymore (...if you know what I mean).

The multi-layered meaning of "puttering" combined with the tendency of older men to turn off their hearing aids has caused more than its share of misunderstandings and has often inspired the exclamation, "I swear to God, Arvid, the wife actually **wants** me to play **more** golf!"

WHEN I AM AN OLD MAN...

...I'll wear
my pants
hiked up around
my armpits...

WHEN I AM AN OLD MAN...

...or I'll let them
ride comfortably
down under
my belly.

The posterior of the average male begins to disappear sometime in his mid-40s; this phenomenon—combined with overall body shrinkage—eventually forces older males to make one of the fashion choices mentioned above in order to keep their pants on (hence the cliché "keep your pants on, old man!").

83

WHEN I AM AN OLD MAN...

...I'll get me one
of them padded
toilet seats for my
private john in
the basement.

84

WHEN I AM AN OLD MAN...

...I'll probably have to hold this book at arm's length in order to read it—not an easy thing to do sittin' on the can, let me tell ya!

By the age of 63, over half of all men read only when in the bathroom, and then only the newspaper, the large-print edition of *Reader's Digest*, or maybe some cheesy humor book about getting old that they received as a gift.

85

WHEN I AM AN
OLD MAN...

...I'll blow my social
security money by
buyin' crap from the
back of books.

Ordering items from the Bad Dog Apparel Catalog shows you have:

  A. A great sense of humor
  B. Great taste in humor books
  C. A limited wardrobe budget
  D. A limited wardrobe
  E. All of the above

Call today for your *FREE* Bad Dog Catalog. It's filled with hilarious tee shirts, sweats, caps and other humorous gift items. Call the number below, or if you're online, check out our cool stuff on the internet:

www.octane.com

We make even the toughest customers smile!

1/800-270-5863

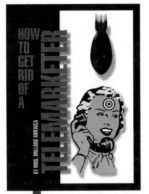

TOUR THE BAD DOG KENNEL

If you're enjoying this book, you'll also enjoy these other books from our kennel.

How to Get Rid of a Telemarketer
Rubber Chickens for the Soul
Who Packed Your Parachute?
The Habits of Seven Highly Annoying People

When I Am An **OLD MAN** I'll Wear **MIXED PLAIDS**

YOU ARE HERE

www.octane.com

humor online

what's bad dog?   bad dog shopper!

humor forum   write to us

A Whole New Breed of Humor Books

When I'm an Old Man I'll Wear Mixed Plaids
Golf on the Tundra
Dictionary for the Skrabble Impaired
Check your local bookstore or our web site for
current titles, apparel, and contests online.

http://www.octane.com

Golf on the Tundra
The Official Rulebook of the
Tundra Golf Association™

by the Frozen Foursome

Dictionary
for the
S K R A B B L E
Impaired

Rare words and
non-sanctioned
strategies for
the crossword
game challenged.

BAD DOG PARODY

Please turn the book over and
start reading at the other end;
the cover on this side of the
book is a bonus cover (provided
at no additional charge).

Just another extra from
the pack at Bad Dog Press!